SPECIALS!

Buddhism

Mary Green

Acknowledgements

The author and publisher would like to thank the following for permission to reproduce photographs and other material:

Page 23   *The Dead Buddha*, Anne and Bury Peerless

Folens allows photocopying of pages marked 'copiable page' for educational use, providing that this use is within the confines of the purchasing institution. Copiable pages should not be declared in any return in respect of any photocopying licence.

Folens books are protected by international copyright laws. All rights are reserved. The copyright of all materials in this book, except where otherwise stated, remains the property of the publisher and author. No part of this publication may be reproduced, stored in a retrieval system, or transmitted, in any form or by any means, for whatever purpose, without the written permission of Folens Limited.

This resource may be used in a variety of ways. However, it is not intended that teachers or children should write directly into the book itself.

Mary Green hereby asserts her moral rights to be identified as the author of this work in accordance with the Copyright, Designs and Patents Act 1988.

Editor: Edward Rippeth   Illustrations: Bob Farley of Graham-Cameron Illustration
Layout artist: James Brown   Cover design: John Hawkins of Design for Marketing
Cover image: David Rose

© 1997 Folens Limited, on behalf of the author.
Every effort has been made to contact copyright holders of material used in this book. If any have been overlooked, we will be pleased to make any necessary arrangements.

British Library Cataloguing in Publication Data. A catalogue record for this book is available from the British Library.

First published 1997 by Folens Limited, Dunstable and Dublin.
Folens Limited, Albert House, Apex Business Centre, Boscombe Road, Dunstable, LU5 4RL, England.

ISBN 1 85276 926-2

Printed in Singapore by Craft Print.

Contents

Introduction	4
Teachers' notes	5

Beliefs and values

Buddhism	8
Where is Buddhism found?	9
The Four Noble Truths 1 and 2	10–11
The Noble Eightfold Path 1 and 2	12–13
Karma	14

Signs and symbols

Buddha symbols 1 and 2	15–16
Bodhisattvas	17
Mandalas and other symbols	18
The Wheel of Life 1 and 2	19–20

Key figures

Siddhartha	21
The Buddha	22
The Buddha's death	23
The Sangha	24
The Dalai Lama	25

Places of worship

Sacred places	26
Buddhist worship	27
A Buddhist temple	28
A Tibetan monastery	29
Meditation	30

Daily life and rituals

Many kinds of Buddhism 1 and 2	31–32
Women and Buddhism	33
Buddhist pilgrims 1 and 2	34–35
The Buddhist point of view	36

Special times

Buddhist festivals	37
Wesak	38
Songkran	39
The Festival of the Tooth	40
A special ceremony	41

Writings

Buddhist writings	42
Siddhartha and the Four Signs 1 and 2	43–44
The swan 1 and 2	45–46
Key word game	47
Glossary	48

Introduction

The activity sheets in this book are designed to make complex ideas accessible to pupils, in years 7–9, who have learning difficulties and are following a course in Buddhism. They are meant to supplement existing courses and are not a course in themselves.

Although the book is concerned with Buddhism, it should be used within a broad context so that a range of religions are addressed. Pupils do not all share the same religious beliefs and should also be made aware that there are beliefs outside religions.

Those who enter secondary school with a history of learning difficulties, usually manifested in limited literacy skills, can bring a profound sense of failure with them. Its effect takes many forms and goes far beyond the academic loss experienced. But, as teachers know, such pupils are not necessarily below average intelligence. The activity sheets, therefore, cover a range of levels and include extension activities. Although they follow a common format, outlined below, they can be adapted to meet individual needs.

The skills involved
Throughout the book, a range of skills are promoted, which follow curriculum recommendations for Religious Education:
- investigation – asking relevant questions and gathering information
- interpretation – drawing meaning from a range of media and religious texts
- reflection – considering and reflecting on beliefs, practices and experience
- empathy – identifying with the thoughts and feelings of others through imagination
- evaluation – appraising issues of religious and moral significance
- analysis – distinguishing between different features of religions
- synthesis – making connections between different features of religion and seeing them as part of a whole
- application – making associations between religious and secular values
- expression – being able to explain ideas, rituals and practices.

The activity sheets
Each activity sheet is divided into four linked sections:

Background
This gives a brief outline of the context and can be referred to while students undertake the activities. Pupils with few reading skills can read the background with a partner and discuss its meaning.

Activities
These are the main tasks related to the topic and may include paired or group discussion, practical or written tasks or refer to sources, the glossary or particular concepts.

Key words
All key words are highlighted in bold and can found in the glossary.

Find out
A greater degree of independence is needed to complete these extension activities. They usually involve investigative work and simple study skills, such as using an atlas and library research. From time to time more sophisticated recording of data using, for example, interview skills is required and pupils are encouraged to work in pairs or groups. A maximum of four pupils in a group is suggested since larger groups can discourage some pupils from participating.

Teachers' notes
The notes are designed to give guidance on teaching strategies and differentiation. They indicate:
- What all pupils should complete and understand.
- What those with fewer difficulties should progress towards.
- When those with greater difficulties would need increased intervention.

Glossary
The key words on each activity sheet can be found in the glossary. This should be copied and made available for regular use, since many of the concepts and terms in Buddhism are complex.

Additional resources
The teacher will need to provide atlases, scissors, glue, colouring pencils, card, pins and note paper, for occasional use.

Teachers' notes

BELIEFS AND VALUES
Buddhism *Page 8*
- All pupils need to understand that Buddhism has no god. They should complete the main activities but will need to have some prior knowledge or access to information on the six main religions. (See *Specials! RE* series.)
- Those coping well could identify a greater number of religions and should undertake their own simple research. They could try to find out what Communism and Humanism are, for example.
- Those experiencing the greatest difficulties should not work alone and should focus on the first three categories of the chart for a smaller number of religions.

Where is Buddhism found? *Page 9*
You may wish to photocopy the activity sheet at A3 size.
- All pupils should try to gain some idea of how far Buddhism has spread and how old it is, before looking into the beliefs and values it embodies.
- Those coping well may be able to recognise that the religion has become intertwined with other beliefs and takes different forms in different parts of the world. Introduce the two principal forms, Theraveda and Mahayana and pupils could then add further information to their maps.
- Those experiencing the greatest difficulties should first identify Asia on a world map, noting where it is in relation to Britain. They should then identify some of the main Buddhist countries.

The Four Noble Truths 1 and 2 *Pages 10–11*
- The Four Noble Truths are very simplified here, but may help pupils to grasp the essential meanings, particularly regarding the loss of desire. The activities focus on three of the Noble Truths; the fourth could be discussed along with the Noble Eightfold Path.
- Some pupils should be able to work independently from the teacher (but with a partner) to draw up a list of their relevant experiences. They could then move on to the Noble Eightfold Path activity sheets.
- Pupils with the greatest difficulties may need to focus on their own experiences first if they are to generalise subsequently. They could list their personal experiences and classify them using their own categories (eg greed, selfishness).

The Noble Eightfold Path 1 and 2 *Pages 12–13*
- As far as possible pupils need to remember the essential points of the Noble Eightfold Path. They should complete the main activity (recognising the circular nature of the eight steps) and record or stick the activity sheet in their books or folders.
- It may be appropriate for all pupils to attempt the extension activities to reinforce what is required to follow the Noble Eightfold Path.
- Those experiencing the greatest difficulties should still attempt the main activity but focus on steps 3, 4 and 5 as they are more likely to understand and relate to those aspects.

Karma *Page 14*
- The teacher may wish to discuss the different Buddhist, Hindu and Sikh ideas about Karma. A comparison could also be made between the Five Buddhist Precepts and the Five Ks in Sikhism.
- All pupils, including those with the greatest difficulties, should complete the main task. The latter may need to explain orally what each picture and comment is about.
- The extension activity could also be carried out by all pupils if it became a drama activity.

SIGNS AND SYMBOLS
Buddha symbols 1 and 2 *Pages 15–16*
- Pupils need to understand the significance of the mudras and the teacher may wish to discuss these before attempting the main activity.
- Pupils experiencing fewer difficulties should be able to research the story of Buddha's moment of enlightenment, when 'he called the earth to witness' by touching the ground.
- For those experiencing the greatest difficulties, the pictures on both activity sheets can be cut out and matched. The meanings will need to be discussed.

Bodhisattvas *Page 17*
- This activity sheet could be used in conjunction with the previous one. The teacher may wish to discuss the meaning and origin of the bodhisattva (one who returns or remains on Earth to help others). The pupils will need to understand the meaning of 'stepping forward' and 'stepping down', which means 'helping'.
- All pupils need to understand that it is the Buddha of Compassion. They should all, including those with the greatest difficulties, attempt the main activities, working together.
- Those coping well should be encouraged to find information about Avalokiteshvara, the most well known of the bodhisattvas.

Mandalas and other symbols *Page 18*
- This activity sheet can be used in conjunction with 'Meditation' (page 30). The teacher may also wish to discuss the meaning of symbols with pupils here. (See 'Signs and symbols' activity sheet in *Specials! Hinduism*.)
- Pupils should complete the activity sheet alone, with a partner or in a small group according to the degree of difficulty they experience. It may also be useful for all pupils to attempt the first part of the extension work and make their own mandala.
- Those capable of simple research should try to find a picture of a vajra, which is held by certain Buddhas. They can use the glossary to assist them.

The Wheel of Life 1 and 2 *Pages 19–20*
- Each pupil should understand that the wheel is primarily a symbol of life's suffering and also that it is continually moving and therefore changing. The teacher may wish to discuss the illustration first before giving pupils the activities. It could be enlarged for this purpose. The outer ring shows the course of a life and the experiences we undergo leading to happiness or unhappiness.
- Some pupils should be able to draw pictures from their own lives without difficulty and might be able to complete a whole series.
- Those with the greatest difficulties should focus on the inner wheel and discuss with others the details and meaning. Pupils may wish to stick the wheel and information in their books or folders.

KEY FIGURES
Siddhartha The Buddha The Buddha's death *Pages 21–23*
These activity sheets could be used in conjunction or separately. They all involve searching for clues from pictures or source material. The activity sheet 'Siddhartha and the Four Signs' may also be useful.
- Pupils should attempt each main activity after discussion about Siddhartha's origins and subsequent life. They should also have some understanding of what enlightenment is. The Background on each sheet could serve as a reminder of the main points.

Teachers' notes

- Those coping well could work independently using the extension activities (and other relevant activity sheets) to compile information on the Buddha's life and Buddhism).
- Those with greater difficulties should focus on the main activities and be given additional source material to examine.

The Sangha *Page 24*
- All pupils should understand that the Sangha is a community of Buddhists and that it is greatly respected. The position of the monks as revered people also needs to be understood. All pupils should attempt the main activity, referring to the background. They can compare answers with each other. (It will be interesting to note if any fail to use the picture clue.)
- Those coping well could investigate the life of a monk further. They need to understand the reasons why monks have so few possessions.
- Those who experience difficulty with multiple-choice questions should focus on identifying the 'true' answers first. The teacher could adapt the activity sheet so that pupils need complete only the 'yes' and 'no' categories.

The Dalai Lama *Page 25*
- All pupils need to recognise that Tibetan Buddhism has particular features and that Tibet's isolation means there has been little significant change. To complete the main activities, pupils need to understand that Tibet is mountainous and travel would be difficult. The teacher could use the sequence of pictures to outline events before pupils begin their diaries.
- Some pupils should be able to investigate why the Dalai Lama is in exile.
- The teacher could use the pictures and comments as a matching exercise for those unable to complete a diary entry.

PLACES OF WORSHIP

Sacred places *Page 26*
- All pupils should be able to identify the principal types of sacred buildings once the main activity is completed. Pupils should read the background and search for appropriate information together. (There are five types of buildings and six pictures. Two are stupas.) They should also identify the countries together.
- Some could complete their own map of Asia and draw the buildings on the correct countries as part of a small project.
- Those with the greatest difficulties should focus on identifying the buildings only.

Buddhist worship *Page 27*
- All pupils need to understand that Buddhists are not praying to a deity. The teacher may wish to read aloud the account of Chang Lai performing puja.
- Those able to complete the series of drawings should be able to complete the extension work. They need to understand the common experiences Buddhists have during meditation. Some may be able to draw comparisons with Hindu puja.
- Those with the greatest difficulties should read the account with a partner, using the pictures on the activity sheet as a guide.

A Buddhist temple *Page 28*
- This sheet could be used in conjunction with the previous activity sheet, since several of the features are the same. Pupils should understand that the shrine aids meditation and that the offerings are symbolic.
- Those whose understanding is reasonably good can find out more about Thai Buddhist temples. There is a famous one in Wimbledon, London, or they may wish to investigate further.
- Those with greatest difficulty should label the drawing and then attempt to identify the symbols with a partner.

A Tibetan monastery *Page 29*
You may wish to photocopy this activity sheet at A3 size.
- Pupils should be able to note the differences and similarities between the Tibetan monastery and the Thai temple. All pupils should complete the main activity without much difficulty. They should then move on to the extension work.
- Those completing the extension work should refer to the activity sheet 'A special ceremony' which outlines the initiation ceremony for boys entering the monastic life or spending time in a monastery. This should be supplemented with information from the library.
- Pupils experiencing difficulties may need to have the information and background read to them. They should try to match the information with the pictures alone.

Meditation *Page 30*
- This activity sheet can be used with the activity sheet 'Mandalas and other symbols'. Pupils should understand what meditation means. Making some attempt to experience it is probably the best way to do this.
- Those completing the extension work might be able to write more fully about what they understand meditation to be. They may also be able to use their words to write a poem. In this event see the activity sheet 'Buddhist writings'.
- Even those with greater difficulties should be able to attempt the main activity.

DAILY LIFE AND RITUALS

Many kinds of Buddhism 1 and 2 *Pages 31–32*
- By the end of this activity all pupils should be able to identify some of the main features of the various kinds of Buddhism. They should also be able to complete a multiple-choice activity.
- Pupils with few difficulties may be able to construct their own questions for others to complete. The extension work outlined should become part of a larger project on Buddhism.
- Those experiencing the greatest difficulties are unlikely to be able to do these activity sheets alone, but once the information is understood they should be able to complete the questions on the chart.

Women and Buddhism *Page 33*
- It is important for all pupils to understand that Buddhists believe in equality between men and women. This is not always practised, however. They also need to recognise that Tara is bodhisattva of compassion. The emphasis on the female rather than the male is to demonstrate that women are as capable of achieving enlightenment as men. She is, therefore, a symbol of equality, motherhood, the helper and love.
- Some pupils may be able to recognise most of these aspects. Others will need to be shown. Those coping well may wish to investigate the experiences of Buddhist women further.
- Those experiencing the greatest difficulty should focus on the picture of the bodhisattva and be encouraged to use the glossary to help them work out the meaning of the symbols.

Buddhist pilgrims 1 and 2 *Pages 34–35*
- The importance of pilgrimage to most Buddhists needs to be recognised by pupils. This sheet could be used under 'Special times' as well as 'Daily life'. They should all be able to complete the map since there are sufficient clues. However, they should check these on a world map to give them a better perspective.
- Those completing the extension work should add the information to the map. They could find out more about Buddhist pilgrimages.
- Those experiencing the greatest difficulty may need to be shown how to construct a key. They should focus on identifying the places indicated, working with a partner.

Teachers' notes

The Buddhist point of view *Page 36*
- It is suggested that all pupils work through the main activity in groups making the appropriate judgements together about the qualities necessary to follow the Buddhist way of life. They could record their answers and compare these with other groups. (The teacher may wish to draw out the main points with the class as a whole).
- Those coping well could identify a range of jobs, occupational and voluntary, which would fit into the category 'earning your living honestly' under the Noble Eightfold Path. They should be able to justify their choices.
- As long as those experiencing the greatest difficulties work in a small group (or with a partner) they should be able to arrive at some understanding of what the Buddhist point of view involves.

SPECIAL TIMES

Buddhist festivals *Page 37*
- Pupils need to understand what a timeline is and be able to create symbols.
- Those doing the extension work will need to research Kathin, which takes place at the end of the rainy season and is a festival for the monks.
- Those who do not understand how to construct a timeline should begin by completing their own, running from birth to present day, marking important dates. They could then attempt the Buddhist festivals timeline with a partner.

Wesak *Page 38*
You may wish to photocopy this activity sheet at A3 size.
- Wesak is the most popular of Buddhist festivals and all pupils should understand that it is a celebration of the most important events in the Buddha's life. It may be useful to remind pupils of what these are. Most pupils should be able to identify the details easily in the main activity. However, they also need to understand the symbolic meaning of much that goes on.
- Those completing the extension work should undertake a more thorough investigation of the Buddha's life and the meaning of Wesak.
- Any pupils who experience difficulty in recognising details should first note the different scenes in the illustration.

Songkran *Page 39*
- Water is an important symbol of Songkran and the teacher may wish to discuss its significance by referring to the background. Pupils also need to understand that saving the fish (and in some places, turtles) and freeing the birds is an act of kindness and therefore in keeping with the Buddha's teaching.
- This point could be pursued further by those doing extension work. They may also wish to compare the 'Water Festival' with the Hindu festival, Holi.
- Those unable to write a diary alone could make a series of illustrations for each day.

The Festival of the Tooth *Page 40*
You may wish to photocopy this activity sheet at A3 size.
- All pupils need to understand what a relic is and the significance of this in the festival. To what extent it is symbolic rather than actual could also be discussed with some pupils. There should be no difficulty completing the main task.
- Those coping well may wish to find out more about Buddhism in Sri Lanka (see 'Buddhist pilgrims'). They may also wish to extend this to a short project on Sri Lanka itself.
- Pupils who have difficulty understanding the more sophisticated concepts should focus on completing the illustration of the elephant. They could then extend the picture to include other aspects of the festival: a large procession with additional elephants, fire eaters, monks and fireworks displays.

A special ceremony *Page 41*
- This describes the initiation ceremony or rite of passage which Buddhist boys undergo. All pupils need to understand this and also that it does not necessarily mean the boys become monks. Most pupils will need to work with a partner but those who are able to write a letter on their own should do so. They should use the pictures for guidance.
- Those coping well could work in groups to discuss the issues outlined in the extension activities. Groups could then compare their findings.
- Those with the greatest difficulties should ensure they understand the sequence of events. The pictures could be cut out, jumbled and pupils could be asked to sort them in order. They could then write a sentence under each picture.

WRITINGS

Buddhist writings *Page 42*
- There is a wide range of Buddhist influenced writing and all pupils should be made aware of this. They should try to tackle both main activities. Clearly some will be more successful than others at understanding haiku. It is not necessary for them to follow the 17-syllable convention, merely to capture a particular moment in their minds.
- Those attempting to write haiku should be presented with a range of examples. They should be told of its connection with Japanese and Buddhist culture.
- If any find haiku too difficult to deal with (though they could all try!) they should make a series of simple pictures or more elaborate covers for those pupils who are writing haikus.

Siddhartha and the Four Signs The swan *Pages 43–46*
These activity sheets can be used in conjunction or separately.
- All pupils should read the stories and understand the plots. 'Siddhartha and the Four Signs' can be used in conjunction with the relevant activity sheets under 'Key figures' (see Contents page). In both stories, pupils need to understand the significance of the Four Signs and their relevance to the Four Noble Truths and be aware that the sheltered life which Siddhartha led meant that he was unaware of suffering. 'The swan' illustrates Siddhartha's tender and caring nature.
- Those coping well should deal with the more sophisticated ideas behind the stories.
- Those experiencing the greatest difficulties should try to complete the main activities working with a partner to make sure they understand the plot and the principal message.

Key word game *Page 47*
A game to reinforce key words. Enlarge to A3 if necessary.
Rules: A game for two players. Tokens and dice will be needed
1. Cut out the key word answer sheet and place it face down on the table.
2. Throw the dice to decided who starts. The highest number goes first.
3. One throw per player unless a six is thrown which allows an extra throw.
4. Players should try to identify as many key words as they can. Players who answer correctly have an extra throw.
5. The winner is the first to reach the last square. The exact number must be thrown to finish.
6. The main object of the game is to collect and remember all the key words. This may take several games.

Buddhism

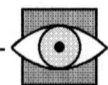
Background

Buddhism is a **religion** which does not worship a creator god. It is a set of beliefs by which people live. This includes a belief that there is another or higher level above ordinary life which we can all reach with the right effort and attitude.

Key words

Buddhism OM
Hindu religion
Hinduism

Religion	God or gods (Tick or cross for yes or no)	Followers	Symbol and meaning
Hinduism	✓	Hindus	 'OM' The sound of creation

Activities

1. Draw a chart like the one above.
2. Write in the names of five religions including Buddhism (the first has been done for you).
3. Complete the chart.

Find out

- Do you know of any other set of beliefs that does not have a god?
- Ask your teachers or parents and visit the library.
- Which religion, if any, appeals to you? Give reasons why.

Where is Buddhism found?

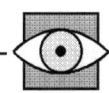 **Background**

Buddhism began about 2,500 years ago. It is based on the teachings or **dharma** of a man called **Siddhartha Gautama** who became known as the **Buddha**. He was born in the mountainous Himalayas in Nepal. Buddhism has spread to many parts of the world over thousands of years but it is mainly found in Asia.

 Key words

Buddha
dharma
Siddhartha Gautama

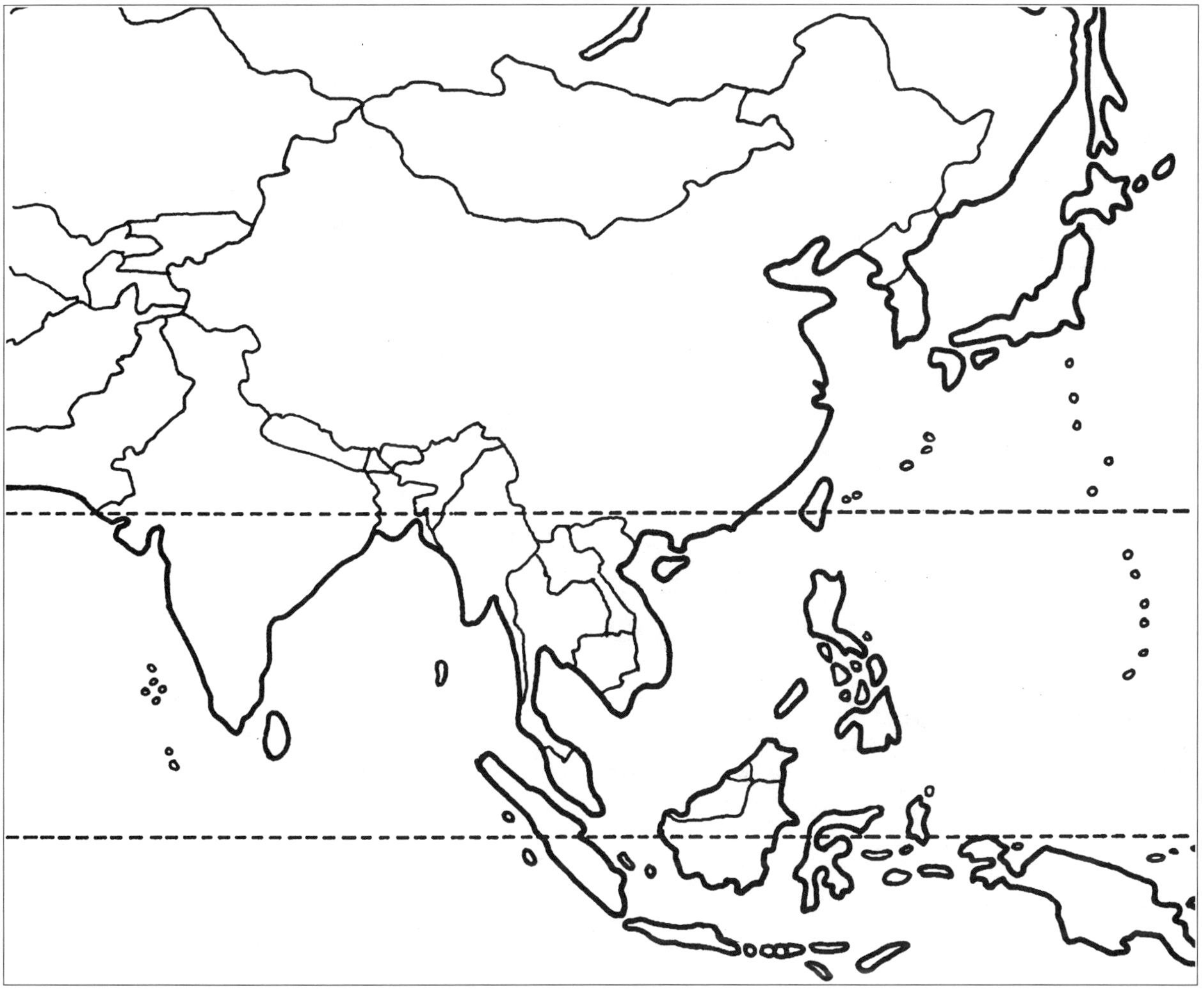

 Activities

1. Using an atlas, write the names of these places on the map and colour them in. They are the main Buddhist countries.

   Nepal   Burma   Thailand   China
   Vietnam Laos   Korea   Cambodia
   Malaysia Japan   Sri Lanka

2. Find, label and shade on your map the regions of Tibet and Kashmir. Which countries are they part of?

 Find out

- There is more than one kind of Buddhism.
- Find out the names of two different kinds of Buddhism and where they are found.

© Folens (copiable page)   SPECIALS! *Buddhism*

The Four Noble Truths 1

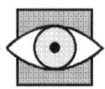 **Background**

The Buddha taught that by understanding what makes us unhappy we can change for the better. He called this the **Four Noble Truths**.

 Key words

desire
Four Noble Truths
Middle Way
suffering

Suffering
We all feel pain and hurt throughout life. Even when we are happy we feel it can't last.

Wanting
We suffer because we long for or desire things. When we get what we want we are not satisfied. Wanting only makes us unhappy.

Losing desire
If we can learn to enjoy life without wanting or desiring, we can learn to be happy and peaceful.

The way to happiness
Life can change for us if we think and act differently. To do this we should not have too much or too little of something. We should keep a balance and follow the Middle Way.

10   SPECIALS! *Buddhism*   © Folens (copiable page)

The Four Noble Truths 2

 **Activities**

Look at each picture below.
1. Match it to one of these three **Noble Truths** – **suffering**, wanting or losing **desire**.
2. Check your answers with a partner.

 Find out

Work with a partner.
- Think of examples of the first two Noble Truths in your own life.
- Talk about why they made you unhappy.
- Together think about the third Noble Truth. Do you agree with the Buddha's teaching?

The Noble Eightfold Path 1

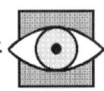 **Background**

Buddhists believe that if you follow a special code of behaviour you will find real happiness. This code is called the **Noble Eightfold Path** because it has eight parts which help you to think and act clearly.

 Key words

Buddhist
Noble Eightfold Path

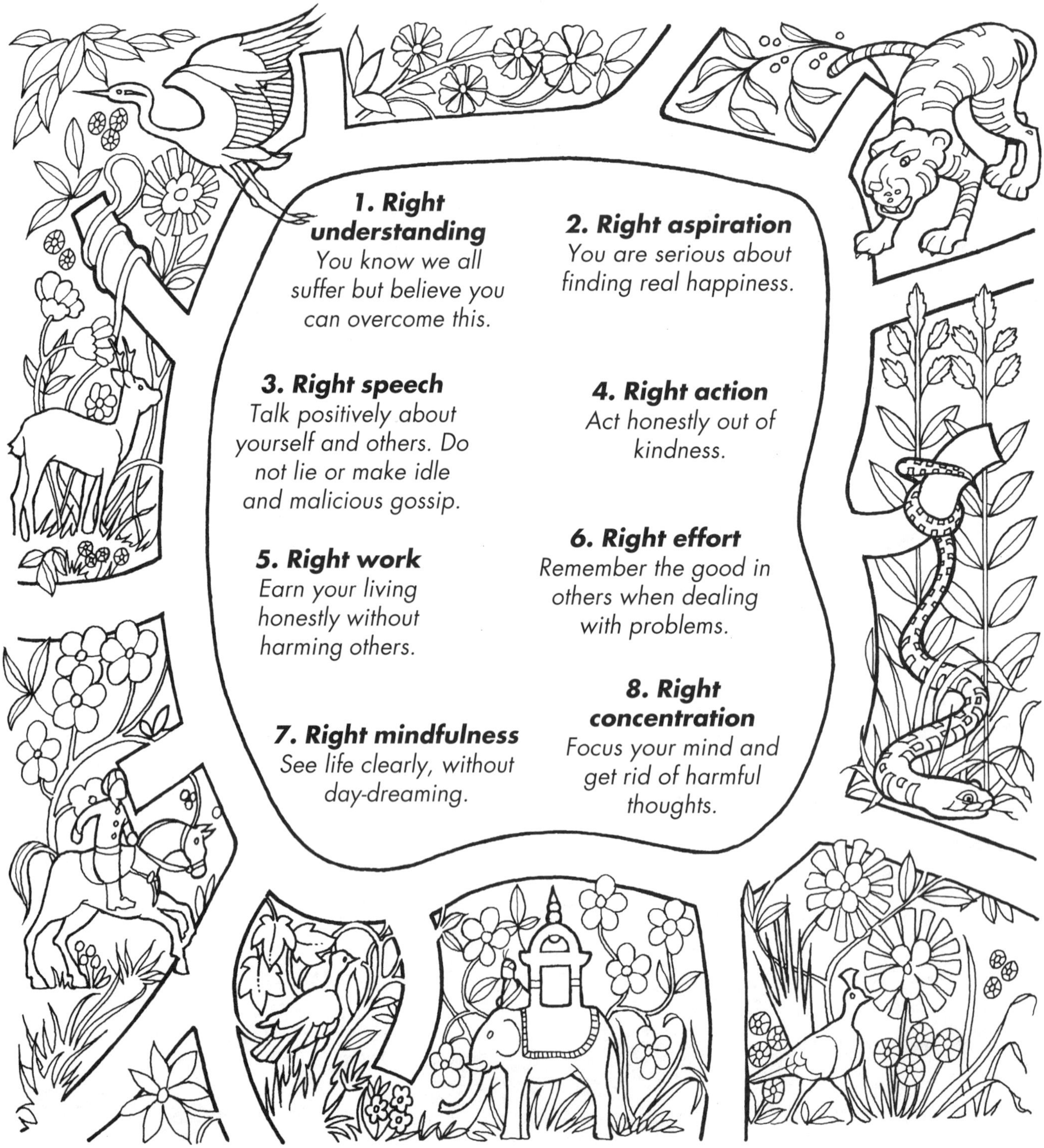

1. Right understanding
You know we all suffer but believe you can overcome this.

2. Right aspiration
You are serious about finding real happiness.

3. Right speech
Talk positively about yourself and others. Do not lie or make idle and malicious gossip.

4. Right action
Act honestly out of kindness.

5. Right work
Earn your living honestly without harming others.

6. Right effort
Remember the good in others when dealing with problems.

7. Right mindfulness
See life clearly, without day-dreaming.

8. Right concentration
Focus your mind and get rid of harmful thoughts.

The Noble Eightfold Path 2

 **Activities**

Look at the Noble Eightfold Path on page 12. Then look at the pictures below.
- Decide which is step 1 on the Noble Eightfold Path.
- Write in the number and heading.
- Now complete all the other steps in the same way.
- Check your answers with your teacher.
- With a partner take it in turns to explain what each step means.

 Find out

- In a group make up a play or write a script about someone who is unkind and changes.
- Link it to steps 3, 4, and 5 of the Noble Eightfold Path.

Karma

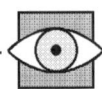 **Background**

Buddhists believe that any action you take has many results. So, if you do something kind you not only help others – you feel happy yourself. Those close to you, such as your parents or teachers, will also be pleased. Good and bad actions and their results are called **karma**.

 Key words

Buddhists
karma

Not to take something that doesn't belong to you.

Not to harm living things.

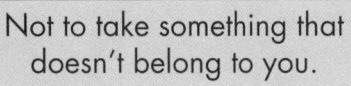
Not to take drugs and alcohol.

Not to speak unkindly about others or lie.

Not to be unfaithful to your partner.

 Activities

Look at the pictures and read the captions.
1. Buddhists make five promises, to help themselves be good.
2. Match each picture to the correct promise to find out what they are.
3. Discuss with your partner which of these promises they agree with.

 Find out

Work with a partner.
- Choose one of the following actions:
  – stealing from a local shop
  – helping a friend find a lost pet
  – spreading gossip about a friend.
- Draw a series of pictures about what happens and who is helped or hurt.

Buddha symbols 1

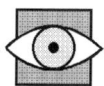 ## Background

Statues and paintings of the Buddha are often very different. They can be male or female, large, small, made of gold, clay or other materials. Sometimes they show the real Buddha, but usually they are **symbols** of the Buddha's teaching. The way the hands are held is important because the hand positions have special meanings. These are called **mudras**.

 ## Key words

meditation
mudra
symbol

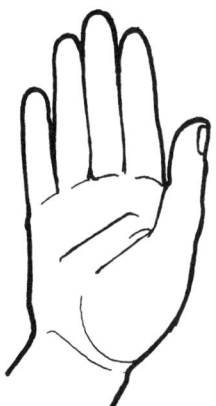

Reassurance

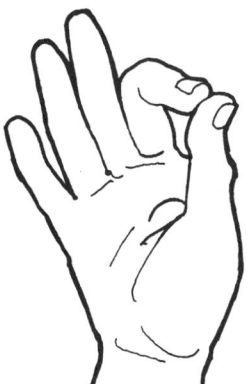

Teaching

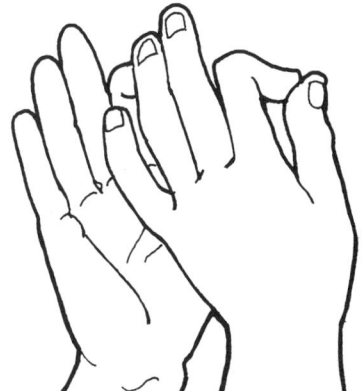

Preaching – turning the wheel of the dharma

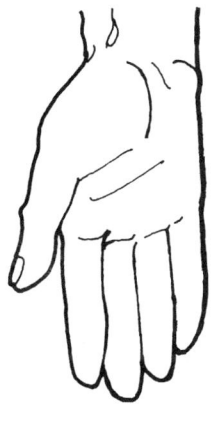

Giving charity

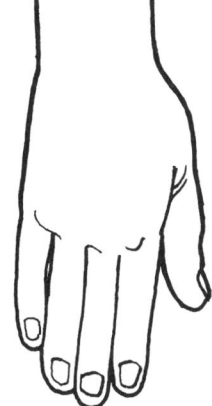

Enlightenment – touching the earth

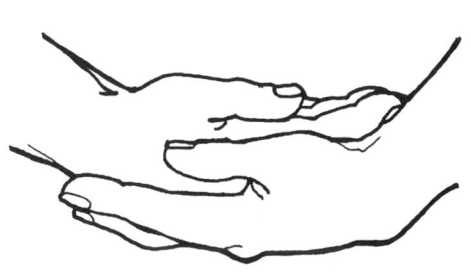

Meditation

 ## Activities

Look at the hand signals and what they mean.
1. Now work out what each picture of the Buddha on page 16 means. Write a sentence about each one.
2. Check your answers with a partner.

 ## Find out

- Why does the Buddha's hand touch the ground?
- Find out the story behind this.

© Folens (copiable page)   SPECIALS! *Buddhism*

Buddha symbols 2

Bodhisattvas

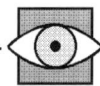 ## Background

In the early days of Buddhism holy men who **devoted** their lives to others became known as **bodhisattvas**. It was believed that after death such people returned to carry out their work. So, the bodhisattva became a symbol of kindness, **mercy** and protection. A bodhisattva is sometimes called a Buddha of **compassion**.

 ## Key words

bodhisattva
compassion
devote
flask
mercy
willow

Sometimes he is seen stepping forwards. What does this mean?

*Sometimes he carries a **willow** branch and a **flask**. Check why.*

 ## Activities

Work with a partner.
1. Look at the three pictures of the bodhisattva.
2. How do they show what he is a symbol of?
3. Use the activity sheet 'Buddha symbols' and the glossary to help you.

 ## Find out

- Look in the library for more pictures of Buddhas and bodhisattvas.
- Try to work out what they could mean.

Mandalas and other symbols

Background

There are many **symbols** in Buddhism. A **mandala** is usually shown as a circle inside a square filled with shapes and figures. **Tibetan monks** paint beautiful mandalas or make them from coloured sand. The colours have special meanings. Red is for the Buddha's kindness, blue for his teaching and white means **purity**. Mandalas are used to help focus the mind during **meditation**.

A Mandala

These three are the Buddha, the Buddha's teaching and the Buddhist community.

This shell is the symbol of the spoken word.

Key words

conch
lotus flower
mandala
meditation
monk
purity
symbols
Tibetan
Triple Jewel
vajra

A. The **conch**

B. The **Triple Jewel**

C. The **lotus flower**

D. The wheel

This flower is a symbol of teaching and purity.

This has eight parts which show the eightfold path.

Activities

Look at the symbols A to D above.
1. Match the symbols to their meanings.
2. Colour them red, blue or white. Choose your colours to suit the symbols and say why you have chosen them.

Find out

- Make your own mandala using pens, pencils or coloured paper.
- What is a **vajra**?
- What is it a symbol of?
- Where can it be found?

The Wheel of Life 1

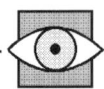 **Background**

The **Wheel of Life** is a **symbol** for the many ways we lead our lives. In the middle of the eight segments of the wheel is the **Buddha**. This reminds **Buddhists** that they can become better people through the Buddha's teaching.

 Key words

Buddha
Buddhist
symbol
The Wheel of Life

1. *The gods are kind, honest people.*

2. *The giants are people who fight and quarrel.*

3. *There are people in great pain.*

4. *The hungry ghosts always want more.*

5. *The animals are people who do not think very much.*

6. *Sometimes people lead happy, thoughtful lives.*

7. *The snake means hate and anger, the cockerel means greed and desire, the pig means ignorance.*

8. *On the outer edge are different parts of a person's life.*

9. *The Wheel is held by the Lord of Death because death comes to us all.*

 **Activities**

Work with a partner. Look carefully at the Wheel of Life over the page.
1. Read the statements 1–9 about the Wheel of Life.
2. Between you, decide which statement refers to which part of the Wheel.
3. Then think of four questions to ask your partner about the Wheel. Swap over.

 Find out

- Draw two pictures of your own life which would fit into the outer edge of the Wheel.

The Wheel of Life 2

Siddhartha

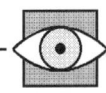
Background

Siddhartha's father ruled part of north-east India. He was rich and powerful. He expected Siddhartha to become a **rajah** like himself. Instead, Siddhartha took a different path. He led a simple life, becoming a great **Buddha** who began a new faith called **Buddhism**. Buddha means **'the Enlightened One'**. This is someone who believes they have found the meaning of life and death.

Key words

Buddha
Buddhism
the Enlightened One
Guru Nanak
Jesus of Nazareth
rajah
Siddhartha

Activities

1. Look carefully at the two pictures.
2. Which is Siddhartha and which is the Buddha? How can you tell?
3. Make a list of the differences. Think about:
   – their expressions
   – their movements
   – what they are wearing.

Find out

- Who are **Jesus of Nazareth** and **Guru Nanak**?
- What religions do they belong to?
- How are they similar to the Buddha?
- Think of three points.

© Folens (copiable page) SPECIALS! *Buddhism* 21

The Buddha

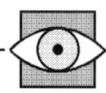 ## Background

When Siddhartha left his father's palace he became a wandering holy man for six years. He owned nothing, had nowhere to live and begged for food. He often **fasted** and became thinner and thinner. But still he could not find the truth he searched for. One day, he decided to sit and **meditate** under a large **bodhi tree**. **Buddhists** believe that under this tree a great experience came to him. They believe he saw the past, present and future as one and understood the meaning of **existence**. It was then he became the **Buddha** or '**the Enlightened One**'.

 ## Key words

bodhi tree
Buddha
Buddhists
the Enlightened One
existence
fast
Mara
meditate
sadhu

*Siddhartha as a wandering **sadhu***

Siddhartha fasting

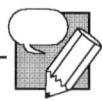 ## Activities

1. Read the activity sheet 'Siddhartha and the Four Signs' (see page 43).
2. Use it and the information here to make a picture story about Siddhartha's life.
3. Write a sentence for each picture.

 ## Find out

- Who was **Mara**?
- What did he try to do to Siddhartha?

The bodhi tree

The Buddha's death

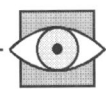 **Background**

After he became **enlightened** the **Buddha** spent the rest of his life teaching. He visited his family once more and then travelled around north-east India for over forty years. His many followers became known as the **Sangha**, the community of Buddhists. He was eighty years old when he died at **Kushinagara**.

 Key words

Buddha
enlightened
Kushinagara
nirvana
Sangha

 **Activities**

1. Why did Buddha travel around north-east India?
2. When the Buddha died he lay in the position shown in the picture above.
3. Talk about the picture with a partner.

Think about:
– how you know the Buddha is dying
– what you think he feels about death
– how this is different from the way others might feel.
Who is the person in the photo? How do you think he feels?

 Find out

- What is **nirvana**?
- Use the glossary to help you.
- How does the picture above show this?

The Sangha

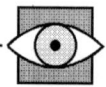 ## Background

The Buddha's followers became known as the **Sangha**. For some Buddhists this means the community of **monks** and **nuns**. For others it means the whole Buddhist community. In the early days of Buddhism the monks travelled around teaching. When the weather was poor they would stop in one place to rest and study. These places were called **viharas** and they later became **monasteries**.

Monks and nuns lead simple lives. They make no money and receive gifts of food from ordinary people. They do not beg. The giving of food by ordinary Buddhists is a way of following the Buddha's teaching.

 ## Key words

monastery
monk
nun
Sangha
vihara

 ## Activities

1. Read the background carefully and look at other information on this page.
2. Look at each sentence and tick the correct box.

		Yes	No	Not sure
1.	The Sangha are people learning to be monks.			
2.	The Sangha can be the whole Buddhist community.			
3.	The Sangha is sometimes shown as a jewel.			
4.	A vihara is a special robe.			
5.	In the early days there were not many monks.			
6.	Buddhist monks sell the food they grow.			
7.	Buddhist monks beg for food.			
8.	Acting kindly is part of the Buddha's teaching.			

The Sangha is the third jewel in the symbol of Refuge

 ## Find out

- Why do some monks carry a string of beads?
- What else are they allowed to carry?

The Dalai Lama

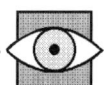 ### Background

Tibet is cut off from other countries by the mountains of the **Himalayas** and so people's beliefs have changed little over the years. Tibetan Buddhists believe strongly in **rebirth**. They also believe in many enlightened beings, some of whom are continually being reborn as teachers. The **Dalai Lama** is one of these. To find out who the new Dalai Lama will be the monks look at new-born babies for special signs.

 ### Key words

Dalai Lama
Himalayas
rebirth
Tibet
vision

The baby can come from a rich or poor family.

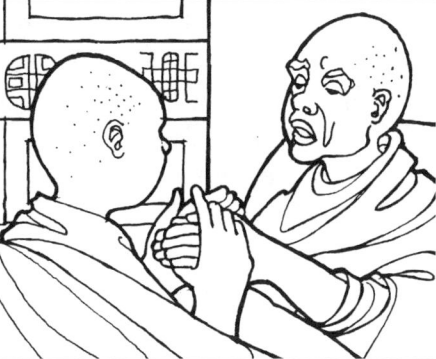

The dying Dalai Lama may say where to search for the baby.

A monk may see special signs in a dream or **vision**.

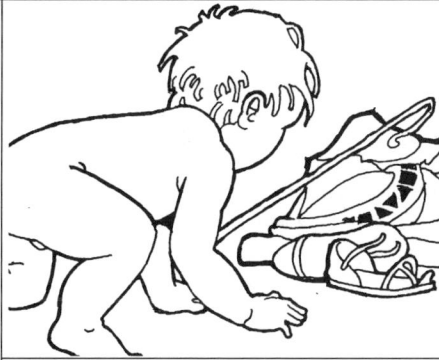

The baby needs to recognise the old Dalai Lama's belongings.

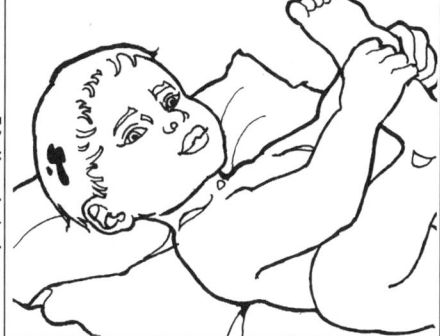

There may be special signs on the baby such as birthmarks.

 ### Activities

Working with a partner, read the information on this page.
1. Imagine you and another monk have set out to find the new Dalai Lama.
2. Together write a diary of your journey for three days.

 ### Find out

- What happens to the baby once he is the new Dalai Lama?
- Do you agree with this?
- Why does the present Dalai Lama not live in Tibet?

© Folens (copiable page) SPECIALS! *Buddhism*

Sacred places

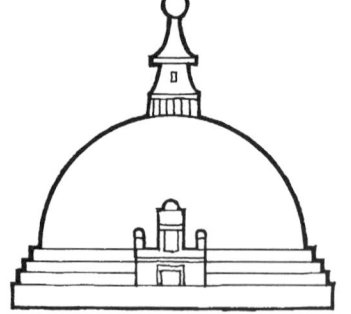

A. _____

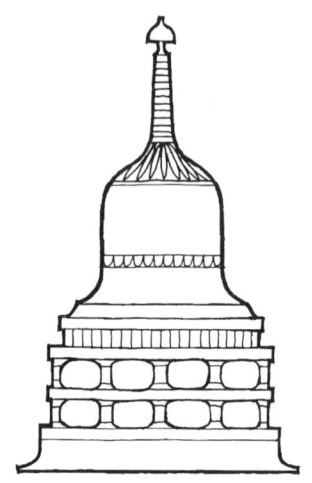

B. _____

Background

There are many kinds of **Buddhist shrines** and **sacred** places.
- In India there are simple bell-shaped buildings called **stupas**. People believe they contain parts of the **Buddha's** body such as his bones.
- In Thailand stupas are taller and decorated.
- In Burma and Japan, Buddhist buildings are shaped like towers, have several storeys and are called **pagodas**. These can be large and part of a temple or small and dotted around a sacred garden.
- In Sri Lankan **temples**, the roofs are flat and the walls are white or cream.
- Buddhist temples also vary. In Thailand they are wonderfully decorated with deep tiled roofs. They are called **wats**.
- The **monasteries** in Tibet are huge buildings made of stone.

Activities

1. Use the background to label each picture with its name and where it is found.
2. Check the glossary if you need to.
3. Check where they are on a map of Asia.

F. _____

E. _____

C. _____

D. _____

Key words

Buddha **pagoda** **stupa**
Buddhist **sacred** **temple**
monastery **shrine** **wat**

Find out

- Find out more about Buddhist stupas, pagodas or temples.
- Make a zigzag folder for others to read.

26 SPECIALS! *Buddhism* © Folens (copiable page)

Buddhist worship

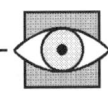
Background

When Buddhists worship (perform **puja**), they do not pray to the Buddha as he is not a god. They focus on the Buddha's teaching in order to find **enlightenment**.

Key words

enlightenment
incense
meditation
puja
shrine

When I visit the temple I remove my shoes first, then go to the **shrine** room. I place my hands together, bow and kneel in front of the statue of the Buddha to show respect. I am always quiet for a moment before I make my offering of flowers. I also light a candle and burn **incense**. I love the smell of the perfume. Sometimes I take a small bowl of rice as well. It is very peaceful here. I sit cross-legged on a cushion to meditate. The monk in the shrine room will ring a bell to remind us when to move on to the next stage of **meditation**. When I have finished I always feel calm and refreshed.

Activities

Work with a partner. Read about Chang Lai, a Buddhist, as he performs puja.
1. Write a list of Chang Lai's actions during puja. Use the glossary to help you.
2. Draw small pictures for each of the actions on your list.
3. Take it in turn to explain your list.
4. Why does he bow and kneel?
5. What does the ringing bell mean?

Find out

- Why do you think Chang Lai removes his shoes?
- Note all the things that happen during puja.
- Say what they mean.

A Buddhist temple

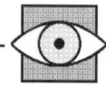
Background

In Thailand, Buddhist temples are called **wats**. They are found everywhere, even in small villages. Wats are usually looked after by local **monks** and visitors may spend the night there.

Key words

gong
incense stick
meditation
monk
scripture
shrine
tanka
wat

A. Parts of a Buddhist temple

1. Buddha statue
2. Offerings: **incense sticks** candles flowers
3. Shrine room
4. Bell and **gong** used in meditation
5. Buddhist **scriptures** – a book of teachings
6. Cushions for **meditation**

B. Meanings for offerings
Good actions spread everywhere like perfume
The light of knowledge
We all fade and die

Activities

1. Label the drawing of the wat using the information in boxes **1–6**.
2. Look at source **B**. Which offering matches each meaning – incense stick, candles or flowers?

Find out

- What is a **tanka**?
- Where are they found?
- What are they symbols of?

A Tibetan monastery

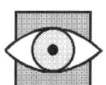

Background

The **monasteries** in Tibet are lively, colourful places. The **monks** and religious teachers are called **lamas**. Boys can train to become lamas from an early age. They live in the monastery and go home to visit their parents for short holidays.

Key words

butter lamp
chorton
cymbal
khata
lama
monastery
monk
prayer flag
prayer wheel
tanka

Lamas
Tibetan monks who wear red robes

Tankas
Large, bright wall hangings

Prayer wheels
There are several of these on a frame. They have prayers on them and revolve by hand.

Cymbals
Played during worship

Prayer flags
Prayers written on cloths and hung like flags

Butter lamp
Lamps filled with butter instead of oil

Chorton
These sit on the altar. They contain prayers and relics.

Khata
A white scarf given as an offering

Activities

1. Look very carefully at the picture of a Tibetan monastery.
2. Read the information with a partner.
3. Then label the picture.

Find out

- Check in the library to find information about the life of a young Buddhist monk.

Meditation

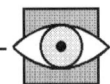 **Background**

Buddhists believe that to gain the most from life we should learn to be **calm**. We should train our minds to be still and free from too many thoughts. **Meditation** is deep, quiet thinking which helps to achieve this.

 Key words

Buddhist
calm
meditation

 **Activities**

Follow these directions for meditating.
1. Find a quiet spot and sit cross-legged on the floor.
2. Breathe normally.
3. Count your breaths up to ten then begin again.
4. Feel your breath going in and out of your body.
5. Focus on this for a few minutes.
6. Now discuss with a friend how you felt.
7. Think of a time when you have been unable to get things done properly because you have been:
    – worried
    – too busy
    – in a bad mood.
8. Describe it to your friend.
9. How might meditation have helped? Think of three points.

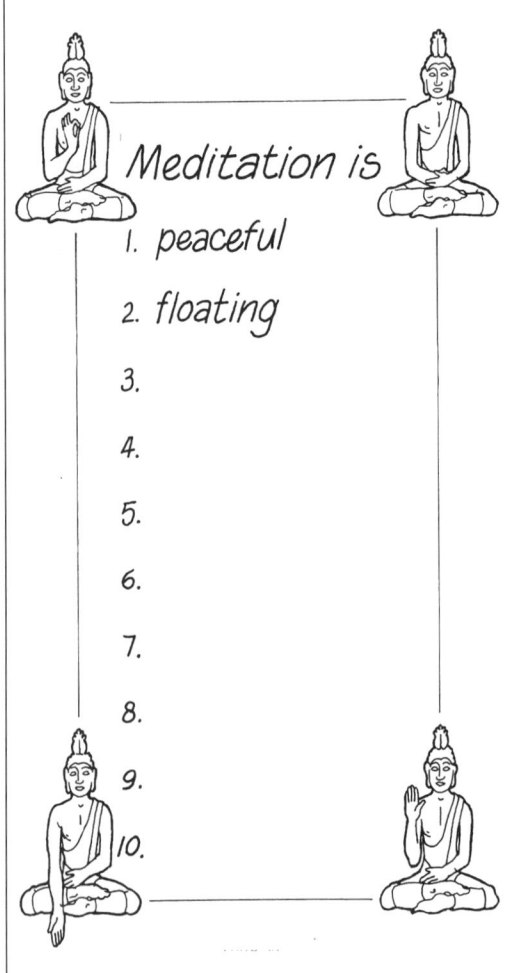

Meditation is
1. peaceful
2. floating
3.
4.
5.
6.
7.
8.
9.
10.

 Find out

- Complete the list with eight more words that describe meditation.
- Use a dictionary to help you.
- Why do you think people sit cross-legged on the floor to meditate?
- There are clues on this page.

Many kinds of Buddhism 1

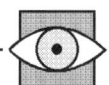 **Background**

Buddhists believe that each person must find their own way to enlightenment, so there are many kinds of Buddhism.

Theravada
One of the oldest forms of Buddhism. It has many monks in Nepal, Sri Lanka, Thailand and Burma.

Mahayana
It means 'Great Vehicle' and is another of the oldest kinds of Buddhism.

Tibetan
The Dalai Lama is the leader, but lives in exile, away from Tibet.

Zen
Found mainly in Japan though it began in China. Meditation is the key to this Buddhism.

Pure Land
This is the belief that Amida Buddha (light and growth) will help to find a 'pure land', free from trouble.

Western Buddhism
Buddhism has spread from Asia to the West. There are now many Buddhists in Britain.

 **Activities**

Read the information and look at the pictures on this page.
- Complete the chart on page 32 by ticking the correct boxes. (You can tick more than one box for each question.)

Many kinds of Buddhism 2

	Theravada	Mahayana	Tibetan	Zen	Pure Land	Western
This means Great Vehicle						
Found mainly in Japan						
The Dalai Lama is their leader						
Two of the oldest kinds of Buddhism						
A new kind of Buddhism						
Amida Buddha will find this for Buddhists						
Their leader lives in exile						
This began in China						
This is found in Britain						
There are no troubles here						

Key words

Amida Buddha
exile
Mahayana
Pure Land
Theravada
Tibetan Buddhism
Western Buddhism
Zen

Find out

- Work with a partner.
- Choose one kind of Buddhism and find out more about it.
- Redraft your work and present it.
- There are Buddhist temples and pagodas in Britain.
  – Find out where these are.
  – If there is one near you try to visit it.

Women and Buddhism

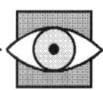 **Background**

The Buddha taught that all people were **equal** and could become enlightened. However, many women did not have the same chances to follow their own paths as men did. Today, there are still some Buddhist countries that do not have **nuns**.

 Key words

bodhisattva   nuns
equal   symbol
lotus flower Tara

Tara is a female **bodhisattva** and is sometimes called Tara the Loving Mother or Tara the Saviouress. She is often shown stepping forwards and carries a **lotus flower**. Buddhists believe that she was reborn many times. Each time she chose to return as a woman rather than a man.

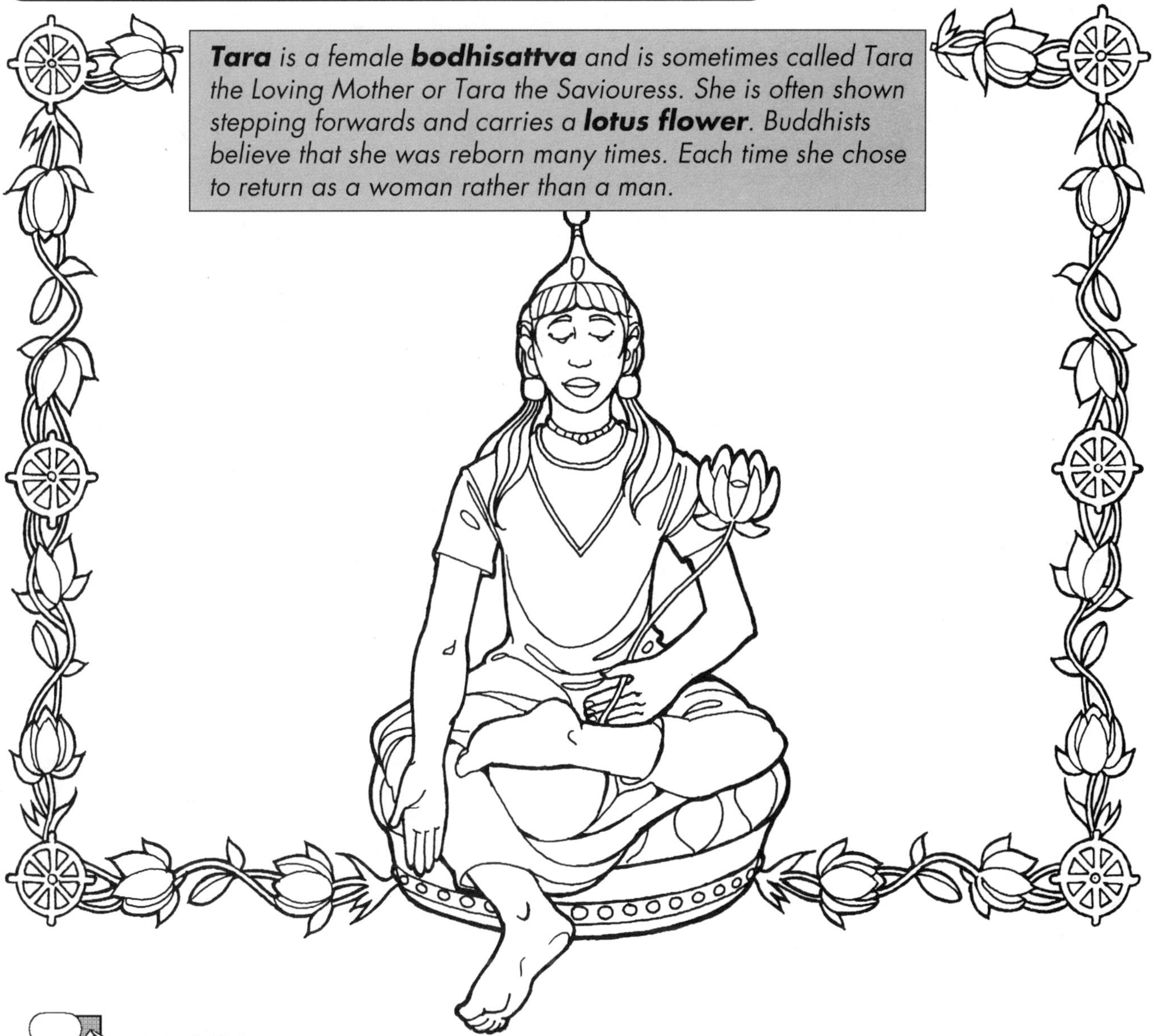

 Activities

**Talk with a partner about these points.
Use the glossary if you need to.**
1. Tara is a **symbol** of more than one thing. What do you think these are? (Look carefully at her movements and what she carries.)
2. Why do you think Tara chose to be reborn as a woman?

 Find out

- Find out about the lives of Buddhist nuns.
- How are they different from:
  – monks?
  – other women?

Buddhist pilgrims 1

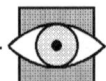 **Background**

Buddhists often visit holy places. They travel to where the **Buddha** was born, where he first taught or where he died. Some pilgrims come from other countries and the journey is one of the most important of their lives.

 Activities

1. Read about the holy places below.
2. Make up a special **symbol** for each one.
3. Complete the map of India and Sri Lanka with the names of the places.
4. Draw the symbols next to them. Complete the key.

Lumbini grove
The Buddha was born here. A stone pillar marks the spot

Sarnath
This deer park is where the Buddha gave his first lesson.

Bodh Gaya
The bodhi tree where Siddhartha became enlightened is here. Underneath the tree is a stone with a footprint. A temple stands nearby.

Kandy
The Buddha's tooth is said to be kept in a temple here.

Adam's Peak
This is a mountain where the Buddha is supposed to have stood. A footprint is cut into the rock.

Buddhist pilgrims 2

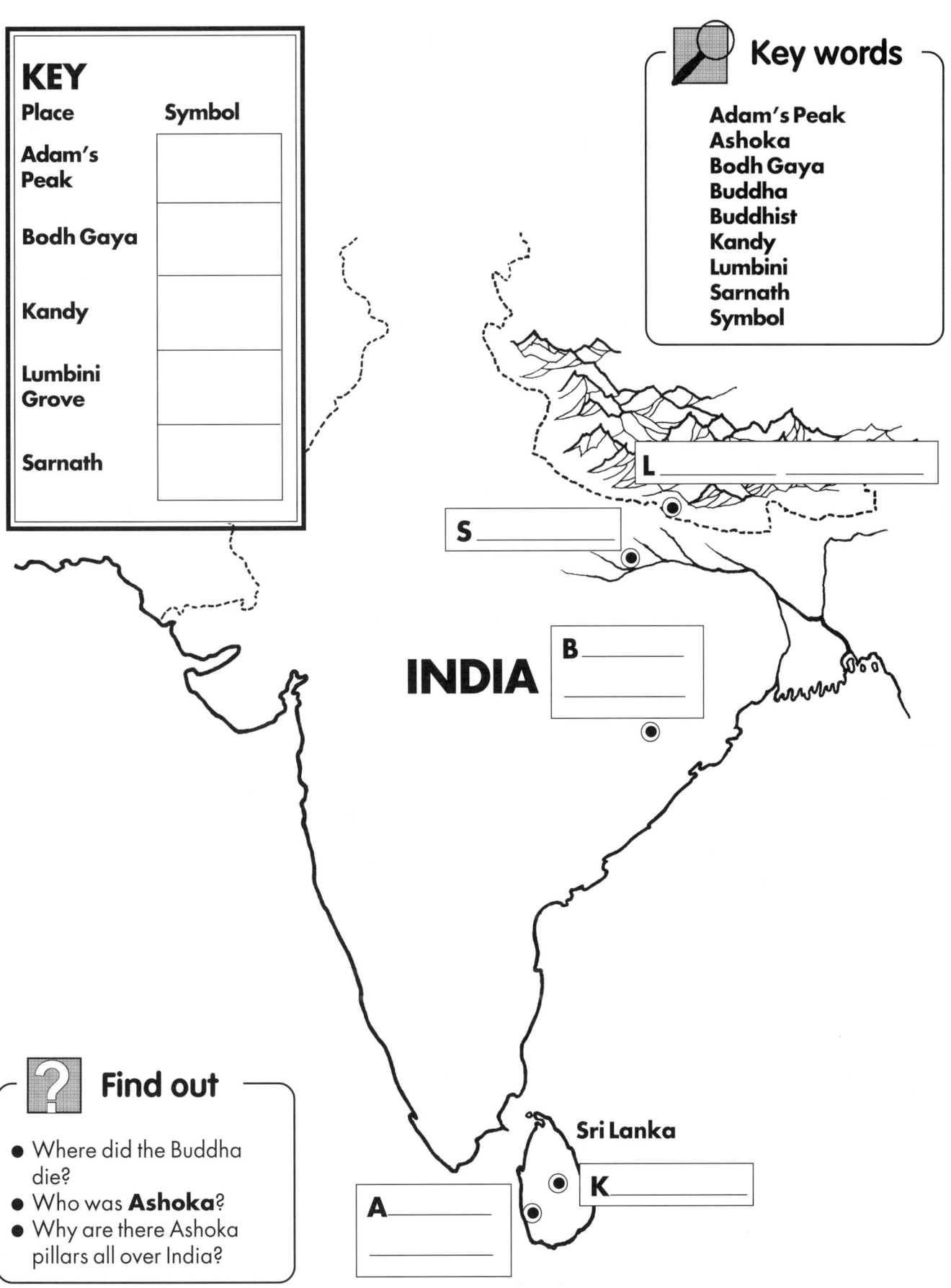

KEY

Place	Symbol
Adam's Peak	
Bodh Gaya	
Kandy	
Lumbini Grove	
Sarnath	

Key words
- Adam's Peak
- Ashoka
- Bodh Gaya
- Buddha
- Buddhist
- Kandy
- Lumbini
- Sarnath
- Symbol

Find out
- Where did the Buddha die?
- Who was **Ashoka**?
- Why are there Ashoka pillars all over India?

The Buddhist point of view

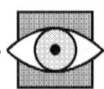 **Background**

To be a Buddhist you must look at life from a certain point of view. This can be summed up in the **Noble Eightfold Path**. These views are often shown by actions taken in daily life.

 Key words

Noble Eightfold Path
Samaritan
vegetarian

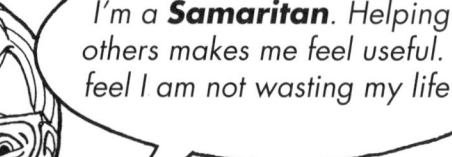

*I've always loved animals so how could I go on eating meat? I became a **vegetarian** about a year ago.*

*I'm a **Samaritan**. Helping others makes me feel useful. I feel I am not wasting my life.*

Money is more important to me than anything. I have a large house, two cars and a boat. I feel a success.

You have to look after yourself. I really believe that. It's no good relying on other people.

 **Activities**

Work with a partner.
1. Decide why these people might or might not become Buddhists.
2. Think about how their views fit with the steps on the Noble Eightfold Path (see page 12).

I'm a gardener. There's nothing better than seeing plants grow and knowing I've helped. I love my job.

 Find out

- Think of five jobs which fit into the Buddhist way of life. Compare them with your partner's list.
- Say why you have chosen these jobs.

I'm always day-dreaming. Maybe one day I'll be a pop star or a great footballer. You can never tell!

Buddhist festivals

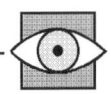

Background

For Buddhists most **festivals** are a way of sharing the Buddha's teaching. How each festival is carried out may change from country to country but the feeling and spirit is the same everywhere.

Key words

Dhammacakka festival
Festival of the Tooth
Higan
Ploughing Festival
Songkran
Wesak

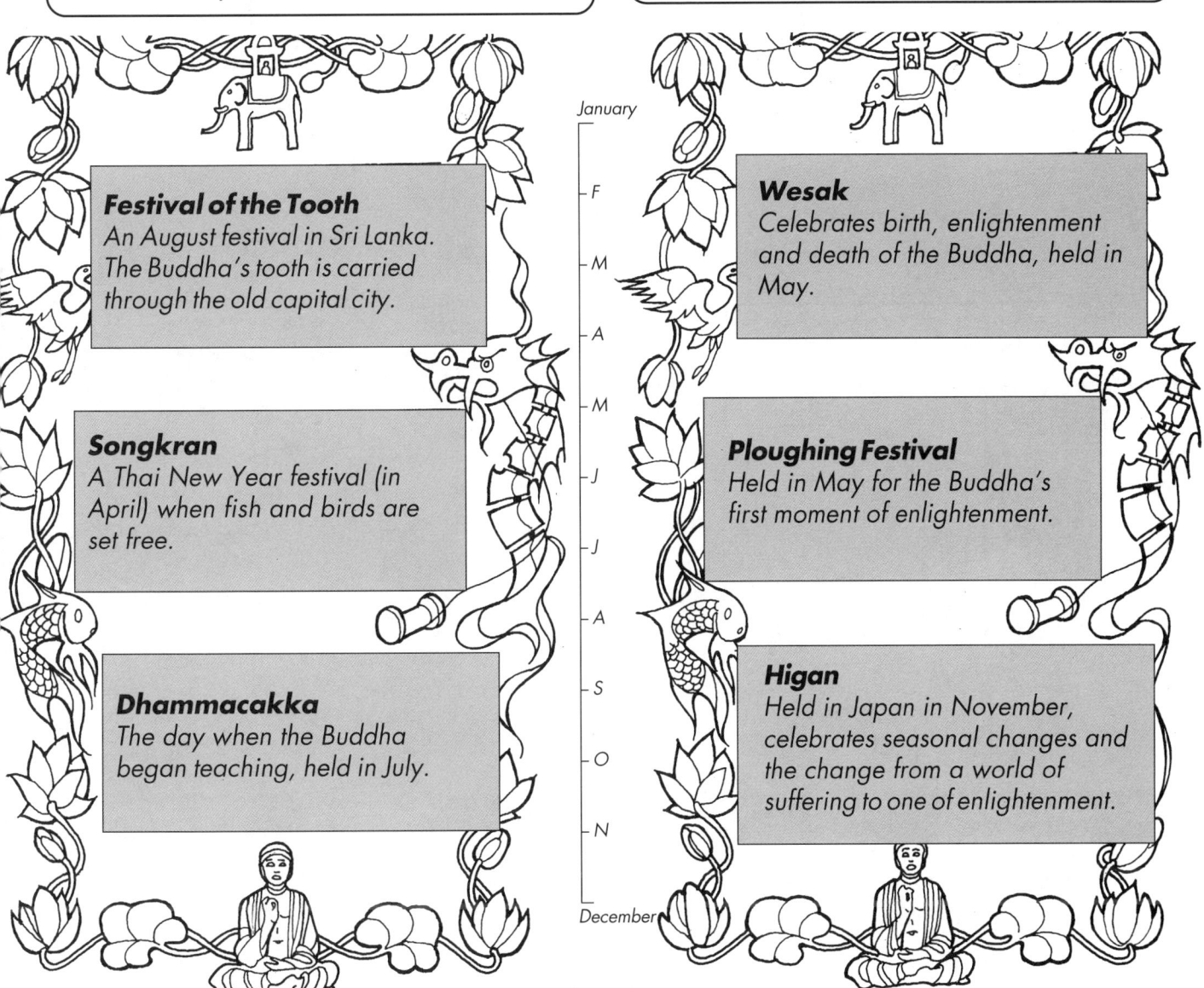

Festival of the Tooth
An August festival in Sri Lanka. The Buddha's tooth is carried through the old capital city.

Songkran
A Thai New Year festival (in April) when fish and birds are set free.

Dhammacakka
The day when the Buddha began teaching, held in July.

Wesak
Celebrates birth, enlightenment and death of the Buddha, held in May.

Ploughing Festival
Held in May for the Buddha's first moment of enlightenment.

Higan
Held in Japan in November, celebrates seasonal changes and the change from a world of suffering to one of enlightenment.

Activities

1. Make your own timeline for the months of the year.
2. Then put the festival names in the correct places.
3. Draw a suitable symbol for each festival.

Find out

- When does **Kathin** take place?
- What happens at the festival?
- What is its meaning?

© Folens (copiable page)   SPECIALS! *Buddhism*   37

Wesak

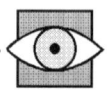

Background

Wesak is the most important Buddhist **festival**. It **celebrates** on one day the Buddha's birth, his **enlightenment** and his death. People attend the temple to give offerings and to hear the monks **chanting**. Flowers and **garlands** are hung everywhere. Sand is spread around the temple and everyone walks without shoes. In the evening a large statue of the Buddha which has been washed is placed outside the temple. Lamps are lit. Scented water is thrown over the Buddha and people walk around it with candles and **incense**.

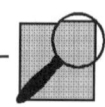

Key words

celebrate
chanting
enlightenment
festival
garland
incense
Wesak

Activities

Read the background carefully.
1. Find all the things that happen at Wesak in the picture above.
2. Label the picture.

Find out

- What three parts of the Buddha's life are celebrated at Wesak?
- Find out more and write a paragraph or draw pictures about each one.

Songkran

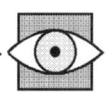

Background

Songkran is a **festival** in Thailand which lasts for three days in April, when Thai **Buddhists celebrate** New Year. Songkran is actually made up of several small festivals. Water is an important part of Songkran. It is a symbol of refreshment and new life.

Key words

Buddhists
celebrate
festival
shadow puppets
Sangkran

The Water Festival
Everyone throws water at each other. There are boat races afterwards. The Songkran princess rides on a white horse. Water is sprinkled over the statue of the Buddha.

Saving the fish
When the rivers and ponds dry up, the fish are rescued and set free in a larger river. Caged birds are also set free.

Shadow puppets
On the last day there are plays using shadow puppets and music and dancing.

Fighting kites
Two groups of kites fight each other in the air.

Activities

Read about Songkran above.
1. Write a diary for the three days of Songkran. Draw your own pictures.
2. Compare your diary with a partner.

Find out

- In what way does helping the fish and birds fit into Buddhist teaching?
- What Hindu festival is similar to the Water Festival?

The Festival of the Tooth

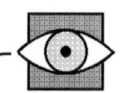

👁 Background

The old capital city of **Sri Lanka** is called **Kandy**. It has a lake, many beautiful buildings and a special temple. Inside the temple there is a **casket** which is said to hold a **relic** – the Buddha's tooth.

The casket cannot be opened and the relic has never been seen, but each year there is a festival to celebrate it. Elephants are dressed in bright cloth and gold head-dresses. These are covered with silver and coloured glass. One elephant carries the casket on its back in a small gold and silver **pagoda**.

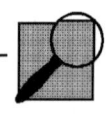

🔍 Key words

casket
Kandy
pagoda
relic
Sri Lanka

✏ Activities

1. Colour the elephant in bright colours.
2. Use silver and gold paper for its head-dress and the pagoda.
3. Label the elephant.
4. Write about the festival, explaining what a relic is.

❓ Find out

- Find out more about:
  – the Festival of the Tooth
  – Buddhist temples in Sri Lanka.

A special ceremony

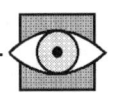

Background

Boys who spend time in a **Buddhist monastery** undergo a special **ceremony**. The story of **Siddhartha** is acted out. The boys are dressed in silk like the young Prince Siddhartha and ride white horses around the courtyard. Then their heads are shaved and they are given yellow or red robes. The **monks** teach them to read and write as well as the ways of the monastery. After a few months, the boys will return home.

Key words

Buddhist
ceremony
monastery
monks
Siddhartha

Activities

Work with a partner. Read the background and look carefully at the pictures.
1. Imagine you are 11 years old and attend a Buddhist monastery for the first time.
2. Between you, write a letter saying what the ceremony was like.
3. Use the glossary to help you.

Find out

- Why do you think Buddhists feel it is good for young boys to attend a monastery?
- What do you think they learn?
- Think of three reasons and write about them.
- Find out if there are the same chances for girls.

© Folens (copiable page)   SPECIALS! *Buddhism*   41

Buddhist writings

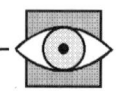

Background

About 500 years after the **Buddha** died, his teaching was written down on large leaves packed together. Later, books were decorated with beautiful pictures. The most important books are called **The Three Baskets of the Law**. The second of these is the most popular. It contains stories said to have been spoken by the Buddha.

Key words

Buddha **Zen**
haiku
Jataka Tales
The Three Baskets of the Law

Activities

Look at the Buddhist book cover.

1. Some kinds of Buddhism such as **Zen** believe imagination can open the mind. Poetry such as **haiku** helps to do this.
2. Read this haiku by Matsuo Basho and write it on the lines below.

   All day long
   yet not long enough for the skylark
   singing and singing.

3. Shut your eyes and imagine a picture of the skylark singing. Think of some simple pictures of your own.
4. Make your own book cover for the haiku, using your pictures and Buddhist symbols which suit the haiku.

Find out

- Find more examples of haikus.
- Try to write your own haiku using your ideas **or** write several haikus and make your own cover from them.
- What are the **Jataka Tales**?
- Try to find stories from this collection.

Siddhartha and the Four Signs 1

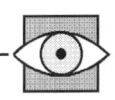

👁 Background

When Siddhartha was born, his father, the Rajah, called the palace fortune-tellers together. He wanted to know what his son's future would be. They looked carefully at the baby, consulted each other and made two prophecies. Siddhartha could follow in his father's footsteps and become king or he would see four important signs. These would change his life forever. He would leave the palace to become a holy man and eventually a great Buddha.

The Rajah was afraid. He did not want to lose his son. So the young prince led a protected childhood within the palace walls. When he came of age he married his beautiful cousin Yasodhara. They had one son.

But Siddhartha was not happy. His life was narrow. He knew nothing of the real world. His curiosity grew and one night he asked Channa, his coachman, to take him outside the palace gates. After a little while they met a man whose hair was white with age. Siddhartha had never seen what time could do and Channa explained that old age came to us all. The Prince returned home surprised and upset. For three more nights he left the palace. Each night he saw something new and strange. He saw a man's face, pale with sickness. He saw a dead man being carried by sobbing relatives. Finally, he saw peace and contentment in the face of a wandering holy man. Here was someone who had overcome suffering and Siddhartha saw what the course of his own life would be.

Returning to the palace he looked at his sleeping wife and child. He would not see them for many years. He saddled his horse, Kandaka, and rode out of the palace gates. Once he had reached the forest he dismounted, replaced his silk clothes with a plain robe and cut his hair. He then began the life of a simple holy man, struggling to find a way to overcome suffering and to understand what life is about.

Siddhartha and the Four Signs 2

Activities

1. What were **the Four Signs** Siddhartha saw?
2. Hidden in the picture below are the characters mentioned in the story, including the Four Signs. Find, label and colour them.

Key words

Channa
the Four Signs
Kandaka
prophecy
Yasodhara

Find out

- Make up a symbol for each of the Four Signs.
- Write a sentence under each one to explain what it meant to Siddhartha.

The swan 1

👁 Background

As a boy, Siddhartha was fond of nature and loved to visit the gardens in his father's palace. One day he was out walking with Devadatta, his cousin, who liked to hunt. A flock of swans flew overhead. Devadatta lifted his bow and arrow and fired a shot. He struck one of the birds, wounding it badly. Blood dripped on to the white feathers and Siddhartha stepped forward to comfort the bird. He removed the arrow carefully and wrapped the wound in petals. Devadatta was not pleased. He claimed the swan for himself, saying it would have died if Siddhartha had not interfered.

On returning to the palace the two boys were still arguing. Devadatta insisted the bird was his. Siddhartha disagreed.

To settle the matter, Siddhartha's father, the Rajah, said they should consult his wise men, the palace counsellors. All the points were considered and after some time the counsellors arrived at an answer. This is what they said:

"The swan belongs only to itself. Its life is its own. Devadatta had tried to take that life. Siddhartha had saved it. To save life is better than to kill. Siddhartha should look after the swan until it is able to fly again. It should then be set free."

The swan 2

Activities

Tick the correct box to complete each sentence.

Devadatta was Siddhartha's

- brother ☐
- uncle ☐
- cousin ☐

The bird was shot by

- a spear ☐
- an arrow ☐
- a gun ☐

Siddhartha and Devadatta argued about who

- owned the bird ☐
- shot the bird ☐
- saved the bird ☐

The swan belonged to

- the Rajah ☐
- Devadatta ☐
- itself ☐

Devadatta was

- an animal lover ☐
- a hunter ☐
- good at sport ☐

Siddhartha wrapped the bird's wound with

- grass ☐
- petals ☐
- leaves ☐

The palace counsellors were

- clever people ☐
- doctors ☐
- soldiers ☐

The palace counsellors said

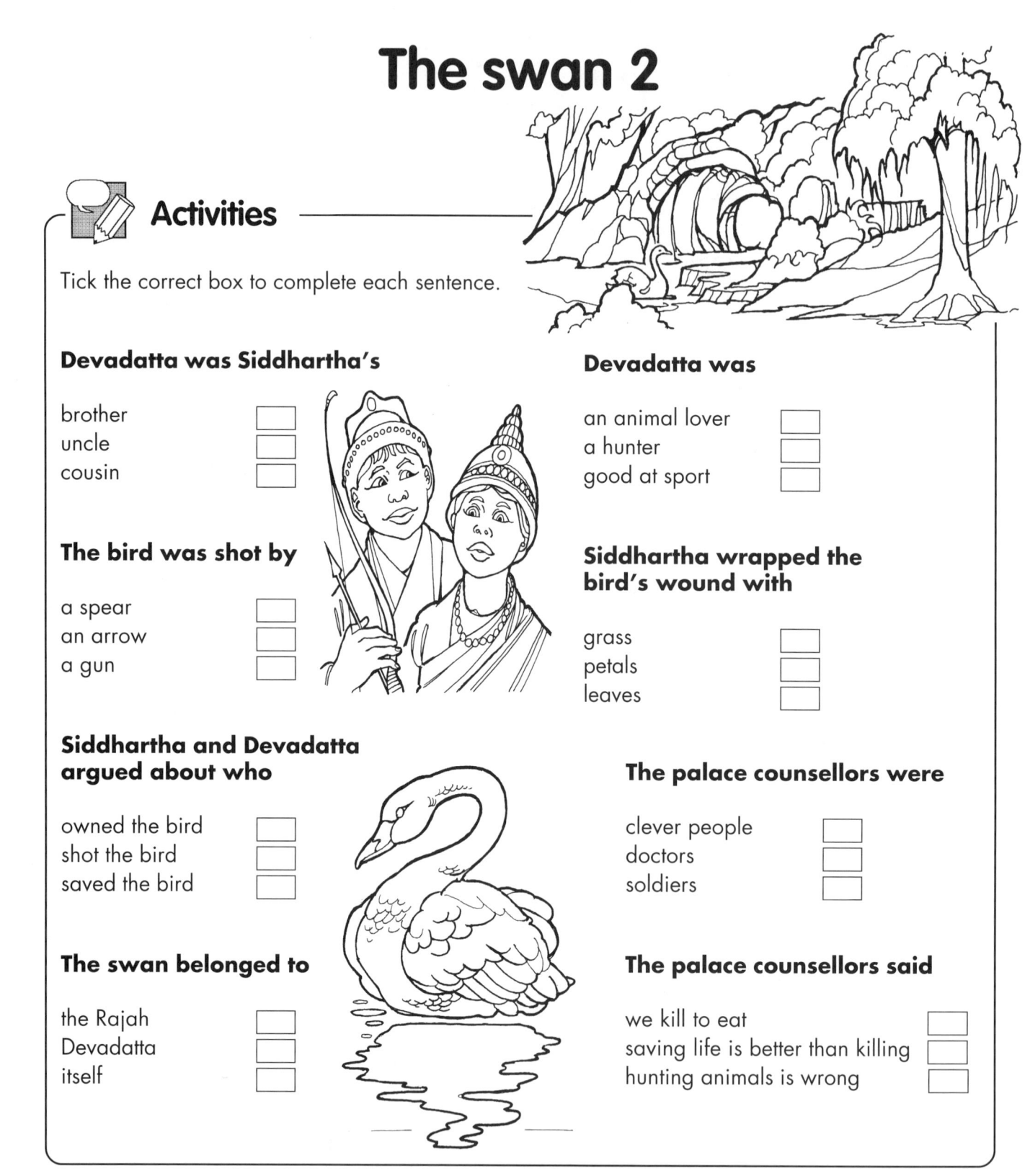

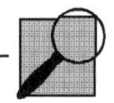

- we kill to eat ☐
- saving life is better than killing ☐
- hunting animals is wrong ☐

Key words

Devadatta
counsellor

Find out

- What does this story tell you about Siddhartha?
- Think of three points.
- How can you tell he is more likely to become a holy man than a king?

Key word game

Key word answers

3. Siddhartha
5. The bodhi tree
8. Dharma
9. Wesak

12. Incense, candles, flowers, food, white scarf (Khata)
14. Prayer Wheel
19. Wat

20. Pagoda
21. Tanka
24. Lama
26. Mandala
28. Meditation

---

1 Start	2	3 Key word — The Buddha's other name.	4	5 Key word — The Buddha's tree.
6	7 Move on four squares.	8 Key word — The name for Buddhist teaching.	9 Key word — The main Buddhist festival.	10
11	12 Key word — Name four Buddhist offerings and move to 17.	13	14 Key word — A prayer in a circle.	15 Go back 2 squares.
16 Move on 2 squares.	17	18	19 Key word — The name for a temple in Thailand.	20 Key word — A sacred building like a tower.
21 Key word — A Buddhist wall-hanging.	22	23	24 Key word — A Tibetan monk.	25
26 Key word — A square inside a circle.	27 Go back 4 squares.	28 Key word — A name for deep thinking.	29	30 Finish

Glossary

Adam's Peak – a mountain in Sri Lanka where the Buddha is said to have stood.
Amida Buddha – the Buddha of the Pure Land. Buddhists who believe Amida has made a perfect place.
Ashoka – a Buddhist King who set up stone pillars across India in praise of the Buddha.
Bodh Gaya – where the Buddha was enlightened under the bo tree.
bodhi tree – the tree under which the Buddha was enlightened.
bodhisattva – one who returns or stays in the world to help others.
Buddha – the Enlightened One, or One who sees everything.
Buddhism – a way of life or religion based on the teaching of Siddhartha who became the Buddha.
Buddhist – someone who follows the teaching of the Buddha.
butter lamp – a lamp which burns butter instead of oil.
calm – peaceful, at ease with yourself.
casket – a small case often holding something important.
celebrate – to mark an occasion or special day.
ceremony – a special parade, show or service.
Channa – Siddhartha's coachman.
chant – to sing in one tone.
chorton – something which holds prayers or a relic. It can be very small or very large.
compassion – to feel for the suffering of others.
conch – a large sea shell.
counsellor – someone who gives advice.
cymbal – a musical instrument in which two discs are clashed.
Dalai Lama – the leader of Tibetan Buddhists who is seen as a Buddha.
desire – to long for something.
Devadatta – Siddhartha's cousin.
devote – to be strongly attached.
Dhammacakka – festival celebrating the day Buddha started teaching (in July).
dharma – the teaching of the Buddha.
(the) Enlightened One – the Buddha.
enlightenment – to understand the meaning of life, the aim of all Buddhists.
equal – the same as.
exile – to be sent away or banished from your own country.
existence – life.
fast – to go without food.
festival – a special day when people enjoy themselves.
Festival of the Tooth – an August festival.
flask – a container holding a liquid and a symbol of healing.
Four Noble Truths – the Buddha's teaching about suffering and how to overcome it.
(the) Four Signs – old age, sickness, death and the holy man, which Siddhartha saw.
garland – a necklace of flowers.
gong – a thick metal disc that sounds when hit.
Guru Nanak – the founder of Sikhism.
haiku – a short Japanese poem which describes a momentary picture.
Higan – a Japanese Buddhist festival held in November.
Himalayas – large mountain range located in India, Nepal and China.
Hindu – a person following Hinduism.
Hinduism – the main Indian religion which believes in cycles of birth and rebirth.
incense – a spice which gives a sweet smell when burned.
Jataka Tales – a collection of Buddhist tales that illustrate karma.
Jesus of Nazareth – the founder of the Christian religion.
Kandaka – Siddhartha's horse.
Kandy – the old capital city of Sri Lanka.
karma – good or bad results of actions.
Kathin – a festival celebrating the last day of monks' retreat during rainy season, held usually in October.
khata – a white scarf given as an offering to the Buddha.
Kushinagara – the place where the Buddha died.
lama – a Tibetan monk.
lotus flower – a symbol of purity and enlightenment.
Lumbini – the place where the Buddha was born.
Mahayana – one of the oldest forms of Buddhism meaning 'Great Vehicle'.
mandala – a picture inside a circle, used to help meditation.
Mara – an evil monster who tried to tempt the Buddha.

meditate – to sit and concentrate deeply so that your mind holds nothing.
meditation – deep concentration.
mercy – to have forgiveness.
(the) Middle Way – to live your life without too much or too little of anything.
monastery – where monks live and worship.
monk – a man who devotes himself to God or the spirit.
Mudra – Buddha's hand positions which convey a meaning.
nirvana – when you are in a perfect state and understand the meaning of life.
Noble Eightfold Path – the Buddha's teachings about the way to find happiness.
nun – a woman who devotes herself to God or religion.
OM – a Hindu symbol, a sound which represents creation.
pagoda – a style of Buddhist temple in the shape of a tower.
Ploughing festival – May festival that celebrates Buddhas enlightenment.
prayer flag – a cloth with a prayer written on it and hung up like a flag.
prayer wheel – wheels which have prayers written inside and are turned by hand to release the prayer into the air.
prophecy – something told before it has happened.
puja – an act of worship.
Pure Land – a Japanese type of Buddhism in which there is a 'perfect' land.
purity – spotless, free from stain.
rajah – an Eastern king or prince.
rebirth – to be born again as a human or an animal.
relic – the bones or some part of the body of a dead holy person.
religion – system of belief, usually in a god or goddess.
sacred – holy.
sadhu – Hindu holy man.
Samaritan – someone who helps those in need.
Sangha – the community of Buddhists.
Sarnath – where the Buddha first taught.
scripture – sacred writings.
shadow puppets – Eastern puppets which are made to cast shadows on the wall.
shrine – holy place.
Siddhartha Gautama – the Buddha as an Indian prince before he was enlightened.
Songkran – a Thai New Year festival held in April.
Sri Lanka – large island country to south-east of India.
stepping forward – gesture of Bodhisattva meaning 'helping'.
stupa – monument to the Buddha.
suffer – to feel pain.
symbol – something which represents something else.
tanka – a large wall hanging found in Buddhist places of worship.
Tara – a female Buddha of compassion.
temple – a holy building where religious ceremonies take place.
(the) Three Baskets of the Law – the main Buddhist teachings.
Theravada – one of the oldest forms of Buddhism, meaning 'the tradition of the elders'.
Tibetan (Buddhism) – the type of Buddhism in Tibet which the Dalai Lama is the leader.
Triple Jewel – a Buddhist symbol meaning the Buddha, the Dharma and the Sangha.
vajra – a symbol held by some Buddhas, meaning strong and hard or powerful.
vegetarian – someone who does not eat meat.
virhara – places where monks and nuns used to rest and which become monasteries and nunneries.
vision – something seen in a dream or imagined, often of great power.
wat – Buddhist temple in Thailand.
Wesak – a May festival celebrating birth, enlightenment and death of Buddha.
Western Buddhism – the type of Buddhism found in western countries such as Britain.
Wheel of Life – a Buddhist wheel which is a symbol of what happens in life and the effect of this.
willow (branch) – a symbol of healing.
Yasodhara – Siddhartha's wife.
Zen – a type of Buddhism found in Japan in which meditation is very important.